DOING BUSINESS ON A DIME

RENAE ROLLINS

authorHOUSE

AuthorHouse™
1663 Liberty Drive
Bloomington, IN 47403
www.authorhouse.com
Phone: 833-262-8899

© 2023 Renae Rollins. All rights reserved.

No part of this book may be reproduced, stored in a retrieval system, or transmitted by any means without the written permission of the author.

Published by AuthorHouse 02/16/2023

ISBN: 979-8-8230-0041-3 (sc)
ISBN: 979-8-8230-0040-6 (e)

Print information available on the last page.

Any people depicted in stock imagery provided by Getty Images are models, and such images are being used for illustrative purposes only. Certain stock imagery © Getty Images.

This book is printed on acid-free paper.

Because of the dynamic nature of the Internet, any web addresses or links contained in this book may have changed since publication and may no longer be valid. The views expressed in this work are solely those of the author and do not necessarily reflect the views of the publisher, and the publisher hereby disclaims any responsibility for them.

This book will teach you how I went
from being a **Hairstylist**, owning
Salons, owning a National Accredited
Hair Academy and Starting the first
BailBond School in the Panhandle!
You will read the strategies I
used to Get up, and Get Started
and building an Empire and
Legacy for my Children.
All on a **DIME!**

TABLE OF CONTENTS

1	GETTING STARTED
8	WILL DETERMINATION & FAITH
16	THE ROAD
24	PASSION
28	RELATIONSHIPS & CONNECTIONS
32	DON'T DESPISE SMALL BEGINNINGS
36	RESOURCES
38	BE YOU

GETTING **STARTED**

Get up, Get Started, and Get Going!

Getting started is the hardest part. Most times we're comfortable in where we are in life, not satisfied but comfortable. Sometimes we're downright afraid. Fear is a dream killer. Someone said, "Fear is False Evidence Appearing Real." We say to ourselves, what if I fail? I say ask yourself, what if I succeed? You will never know if you never step out of your comfort zone and GET Started! Be a game changer, yes, you're going to make some mistakes. Mistakes are a part of the process; you will only grow from them. Don't think of them as mistakes, think of them as lessons. They are only meant to teach you. Just don't make the same mistakes! You can do this! It only takes you getting started, God will send the people, places and things you'll need at the right time. What you have inside of you is unstoppable. The only person that can stop You is You.

There is more to you then working on a J O B. You could never have the financial freedom you want, working on someone's Job. That job is just a steppingstone to your bigger picture. If you hate going to that job, then that job is not your future. Step out and began working on your Dream! I'm not telling you to quit that job right away. Get a plan of action, I call it a "Break Out Plan", The day I plan to Break out of this Hole! Plan your Exit! You might ask "where am I Breaking Out to"? I say to you, you, you're Breaking Out to the authentic You! You're about to tap into a Greater you that you never knew existed!

Once you step out of your comfort zone, new thoughts and Ideas will began to flourish. It's exciting! Sometimes I want to pinch myself to see is it really real! I've learned you must strike the fire while it hot. Meaning when the ideas start flowing you must begin to write them down on paper. Then began to put a plan of action into place. someone said, "it's better to be prepared for an opportunity than to be unprepared when the opportunity comes" You never know when that opportunity will come. Do what you know to do.

Now is your time! Use your Gift.

The Bible says, "Your Gift will make Room for You" It didn't say your money will make room for you. But YOUR GIFT. I personally know this to be true. There's a large Room prepared for you in this world. Make your mark on society. Leave a Legacy for your children & their Children.

To stir up the Gift, you must begin to hone your gift, sharpen it up, take some classes and get the education you need to take the Leap. I can motivate you, but you will have to be the one to take the LEAP! And That's how you'll Conquer that dream killer called FEAR!

God Blessed me with the gift to Style Hair and adorne women and men. I loved what I did. I love the smile I put on my clients faces. This was never my Job; it was always my PASSION! Thats how I got my start! I used the gift that God gave me. The Bible says "Little is much in the master's hand. Think about it, what's your gift?

What is that thing that you do great with the least amount of effort?

Let me tell you that's your ticket out? Use it, strategize and plan your exit.

Getting Started is hard.

It will take dedication, Perseverance motivation, and this is not all. I heard someone say, "You must be willing to do the things others won't do, in order to have the things others don't have. When I started my business, I was the, janitor, the secretary, the book keeper, the stylist, the instructor. I did it all, I was determined to Make my Mark! I had Will, Determination and Faith!

WRITE YOUR EXIT PLAN!
How will you use these tips to Conquer Fear?

GETTING STARTED: EXIT PLAN

WILL
DETERMINATION & FAITH

TOTAL ENTREPRENEURSHIP.
A PEICE OF THE AMERICAN PIE!

These are the main ingredients for Doing Business on a Dime! In my opinion, YES! Its gonna take all three in order to make your dreams a reality. Will is a action word, it is a prediction of what you want your future to look like, it is your desire, choice and willingness, to do what it takes to do what you intend to do for your life. Some individuals are born with a strong will and some are not. But I will definitely say I am a strong willed person. Once my mind is set on something, I won't stop until I have what I desire. This is one on the main ingredient in Doing Business on a Dime.

Determination

Is another piece of the pie. Determination is the act of coming to a Decision. Listen, when you decide to come to the decision that you want to be an Entrepreneur, Only you can make that happen, It would take you, Your body and Your mind. If it's in You to do! It will take you to get it done! Yes, there will be others that you will need to assist you in the process. But ultimately it is your Dream and it will take your Will and de- termination to get it it done. Please don't think that, going into your own Business, gives you the luxury of getting up out the bed when you want, going to bed anytime you want, No it is is the opposite. You will have to be the first one up and the last to go to bed. You will be the the first to get there and the last to leave.That's if you want to be successful on this Journey of Becoming an Entrepreneur.

Faith

Although I'm mentioning this last, trust me, this will be the Rock of all your endeavors. It will take YOUR Faith. Faith is the substance of things hope for and the evidence of things not seen. In other words you will have to See it, BEFORE you See it. You got to see it in your mind, you got to believe that you can achieve it, in your heart. Let me give you a picture of what I'm talking about. My daughter and I walked in to a building I was thinking of buying to put my school in the building looked desolate and depressing almost to be abandoned, when we walked in, my daughter was immediately turned off. But I begin to see the classroom, the lunch room, where the sinks would go, the design to the ceilings and the floor, I seen where my office would go. I seen it in my minds eye. And I'll tell you the truth, My credit was no good, but I was walking by Faith, I didn't have the money, but I kept walking by Faith, I was looking for building to buy in spite of the fact I did not have money, nor good credit, I had an unction in my belly that was telling me now is the time, you must move NOW.

I had Faith that it was God speaking to me. Yes this was a small ran down building on a main highway but when I walked in that building, I knew it was mine. That's what I mean by having Faith in God and your Dreams! I was turned down by a few banks, and then I remembered I had met a gentlemen years ago that worked for the Black Business Investments.Corp. I tracked him down and sure enough, with my low credit score, no money in my pocket or my bank account,

THE DOOR WAS OPEN!

Another step in Faith! I was able to get the deal done, I'm not telling you nothing I read or heard on TV I'm telling you what I lived, and I know if I can do it, a little girl out of North Philly, who come out from drug pushers, drug users, no college education, then I know YOU CAN DO IT.

Once

I bought the place and began the work, the finished work looked exactly like what I had seen in my mind. Thats what I mean by you got to SEE it before you SEE it. It would take place in your mind first, and then when you take action you will see it COME ALIVE. But don't be fooled, YOU have to see it, many people may see it for you, your mother, your friends and to be truthful even your enemies may see the Gift in you, but until you can see your life vision and dreams for yourself, you will never put them into action. BE DETERMINED to bring your WILL and your FAITH Into congruence, put it in to action and watch your life change!

I'll say without faith people, it would be impossible. You will have to believe in yourself to get things done on a Dime. I had no money, no formal education, I am a Hair Stylist by nature, that's the gift God gave me, but I knew deep inside there was more for me, I knew my gift in styling hair could take me further than where I was in my life.

I wanted my piece of the pie and I did what I'm telling you to do. I bought my Will and Determination and extra ordinary Faith together to live together in my house (mind). And this is how I conquered Fear.

I say extra ordinary, but honestly all it takes to begin is a little faith, faith the size of a mustard seed (according to the Bible) in order to get started. Once you start, your faith will grow larger and larger. Because i'll tell you, the larger the dream, the larger your faith will need to grow.

You can do this!

WRITE: WHAT WILL IT TAKE FOR YOU TO STEP OUT?

WHAT GETS IN YOUR WAY? OR WHO?

WILL DETERMINATION & FAITH: STEP OUT

THE
ROAD

Everything I DiD, I DID it BROKE.

I had to have Faith. Let me tell you my story, I have to tell people all the time, I didn't grow up with a silver platter or a silver spoon Or a Rich uncle. I started with nothing, I grew up in North Philly, in what we call the Hood. My parents worked to pay there bills and keep food on the table. When my mom and Pa split, things went hay wire and we literally had to fend for ourselves. Grab a copy of my first book From Pressure to Potential and you can read my story there. I wasn't the smartest cookie in the jar either. What I had was a foundation of faith and prayer. I had a praying grand mother, and somewhere deep inside I knew God was my anchor, He was the one that I could trust and depend on. I was broke at the age of 21. I had family and friends, but they were just as broke as I was.

    I started doing hair, in Philly on the corner of my block or on a porch at about 12 years old. I knew right then, that I wanted to be a hair dresser. By the age of 17, between my sister and a miracle from God I graduated out of High School. I signed myself up in a Beauty School, in Philadelphia, attended beauty school, passed my State Boards, and I began to dream! Not just Dream but Dream BIG! I not only seen myself owning a Salon but I even dreamed of having a Beauty School one day! After seeing the Director of Wilfred Academy Beauty School I attended, how she walked with Poise, her hair was always Fly, she wore these fly glasses and clothes were always pristine. I knew then, that I, would be Ms. Sylvia one day, (smile) that was her name. See contrary to the way people think today, It's ok to see a person doing what you love and begin to watch them, you will know in your heart that if this lady can do this, I sure can. And that's what I believed. The dream was planted in my heart

Then reading Madame C.J. Walker Story I began to have a clear map on how I wanted my life to be! But listen, if I never have taken the first step in signing myself up for beauty school, I would not have ever met Ms. Sylvia. Let me say this, When I left Beauty School, I went into Ms. Sylvia's office to tell her good bye, because I was moving to Miami, She look at me and said, "good bye Renae, maybe I will come and visit your Salon in Miami one day" I said really, I said you think i'll own a Salon one day? She looked over her glasses and said to me so strongly, "I know you will". Wow, imagine that, someone I highly respect- ed, someone I was dreaming to be like, spoke life into me, she seen a Business woman in me. I never told her any of my dream, my God I felt like I was walking on a cloud that day y'all! But listen, if I never signed myself up for Beauty School and if I never had picked up books, such as Madame CJ Walker who was a Slave owner daughter, and the Beauty world made her the first Black Millionaire, had I did nothing, I would never have accomplished nothing, and doing nothing will lead you to Nothing!

Now of course there were plenty of Bumps and Bruises and Hard times, in between, Years of Tears, hard work, and sleepless nights. I was betrayed by people I trusted, and a lot of times I felt all alone in this world. I was married, but single (if you know what I mean). But managed to stay focus, because I had a WHY, and my WHY was Myself and my daughters Reenie and Neisha at the time.

You must have a WHY.

Why are you strong will, Why are you Determined to do what you need to do for your life to change for the better, Why you get up every morning and hope things get better. It's your WHY that's gonna keep you focus, when people walk out on you, talk about you and try to belittle you. It's your WHY that's gonna make you stay the course when you want to walk away, WHAT'S YOUR WHY? I was young, but I was hungry for better. I had Big Dreams and two little girls to raise. I wasn't gonna let nothing stop me, I was DETERMINED to do what I had to do.

I worked doing Hair from sun up to sun down- some days. I ate, sleep and breathed doing business, I had developed a Bull Dog mentally, not even realizing it. You might say, Whats a Bull Dog Mentality, well, think of when a Pitt Bull grab hold to a piece of meat, and you try to pry it out of his mouth, you got to fight to get that meat out, why, because he is Hungry. That's the mind set I had, Im gonna do what I got to do to get where I want to go, and If you try and take it your gonna have the FIGHT of your life. When my son Joshua was born, I invented a Pillow called, My Baby Shoulder Holder Pillow, marketed and sold them. I was determined to BE the Great Madame C.J. Walker of my time! Now I was a Licensed hair Stylist, in 1993 I opened up my first Beauty Salon, In 2004 I opened the Only African Ameri- can Hair School in Tallahassee Florida, and by 2010 My School was a National Accreditate, Beauty School, 17 years now. Never would of thought. The Dream gets bigger and bigger. I also Started the first BailBonds Academy in the Panhandle (Perkins and Rollins BailBonds Academy)!

Who are you prescribing to be like?

Who is your example? It"s okay, You can see someone who will be the example of what you inspire to be. I did. I'm not writing this book because the Road was easy, I'm writing this book to let you know that it was worth it. It was worth it All. I'm 58 now and I'm living my dream, doing what I love everyday. And when you do what you love, it doesn't feel like work. Little ole 'me. I had the Will, Determination and of course My Faith. Faith in God, and Faith in myself. I believed I can Do It! I Believed in Me

WRITE:
WHAT IS YOUR WHY?

WHO ARE THE ROLE MODELS
IN YOUR LIFE?

WHAT ARE SOME THINGS THAT
KEEP YOU FROM YOUR WHY?

WHAT WILL YOU DO TO STOP
THEM FROM STOPPING YOU?

THE ROAD: YOUR WHY

PASSION

Passion according to Webster's dictionary; A strong feeling of enthusiasm or excitement for something or about something.

When your Doing Business on a Dime, meaning you have very little or no money, No investors and No rich friends or Family members. Passion is an attribute you must posses! Find your Passion and you will find your Purpose! You will not only need Passion concerning your gifts and Talents,

In your pursuit to total entrepreneurship you'll need to be passion- ate about what you believe.

There will be all kinds of thoughts coming into your mind at any given time, when you decide to Do Business on a Dime.

You must cancel out every negative thought, that will tell you, you don't have what it takes, that negative voice will tell you, your driving your family in a hole. People will tell you to quit, give up, get a real job. You will have to press pass that negativity.

Block out all the negatives and Pursue after your Dreams of being your own Boss, Signing your own paychecks, and walking in Financial freedom, being in control of your own destiny! I DiD IT, and so can you.

I was passionate about being the Best HairStylist I can be. I woke up early and got home late, at one point I was working in two Cities. I had a Goal in mind, I had a Bigger vision. I started with nothing, but I was Excited and Enthusiastic about my Destiny. I had un- shakable Passion. I can taste being a business women. I wanted that Beauty Salon, I wanted that Beauty School, I went to sleep thinking about it, I woke up with it almost every day.

No, there was no silver platter, no silver cup or spoon, and no rich uncle. I had the ability to Dream and Dream Big! Not only did I dream of owning my own Beauty Salon, I was bold enough to Believe I can open my own Beauty School one day. If at first you don't succeed try, try again. I opened a Salon and had to close it.

I started over and the Salon was a Success!

I started the process years later of open- ing the Beauty School, I failed at it, but I failed forward, believing I can do it! I only had a few pennies and I lost that. They took what little I had and gave me no results. I was discouraged and ashamed, but I was still thirsty for it. I knew it was mine. I kept working as a Hair Stylist and in 2004 opened the First African American Owned Beauty Academy, 6 years later we were, National Accreditate Beauty school, I also went on to open the First BailBonds Academy in the Panhandle, Invented a pillow, and wrote my first Book (From Pressure to Potential). Total Entrepreneurship!

I'm not telling you all this to impress you, I'm telling you this to impress upon you, that your Dreams must be bigger that your Wallet, or your Dreams are two small. Yes I had Big Dreams, and no money. "Everything I did, I Did it Broke" I had to have Faith, I had to Believe

RELATIONSHIPS
&
CONNECTIONS

This is a Must! You will need to foster good Relationships and Connect with the right people, this is important, in any event in your life. I fostered great relationships on my Journey of be- coming an Entrepreneur, I got aquatinted with Bankers, Investors, Executive Directors of Small Business Administrators in my City. I would meet with City Councils, and City representatives in my community. I found this was important. Many clients sat in my chair that gave me great advice. I learn so much from the Client friends that I made in the Hair Busi- ness. Get out of your shell and meet people. Its gonna take great relationships to get you to certain levels of your Journey.

A wise man told me once that you must work on your Business and not in your Business. This statement changed my life. I became a graduate of the Jim Moran Entrepreneurs Institute, which was an awesome experience. Below write a list of Bank presidents in your area, start with the people you bank with, ask for a meeting, if they don't want to meet with you, go to another bank. Seek out the Executive Directors of Small Business in your area Call a meeting with them. Take good notes, and develop your plan. Get your credit on task so you can dodge the high interest rates and the No's.(smile). Seriously, I don't care how many no's you get, don't stop asking and looking, there is a Yes wait- ing out there somewhere for you. And NEVER QUIT, Winners never Quit and Quitters never win!!

RELATIONSHIPS & CONNECTIONS: MEETINGS

DON'T DESPISE SMALL
BEGINNINGS

DON'T DESPISE SMALL BEGINNINGS

While doing Business on a Dime, I started out with all used furniture, I would go to Habit Restore's, buy off of Facebook, was always looking for Salon's that were going out of business. People who got into the business and they started off BIG, brand new equipment and big locations. I would search them out, and when they close down and I would offer them little to nothing for previous purchased equipment they had just sitting in a storage. See the Bible says "Don't despise small beginnings " and when I read that, I knew if I took care of my business when it was small, and if I nurtured it and give it me best It would eventually grow into what I wanted. I taught one student as if I was teaching a hundred. It did not matter if nobody showed up, I showed up every day.

I appreciated the small beginnings because the mistakes I made back then was easier to fix with a few students, than if had a lot of students. I learned a lot during the lean times. Never go out and borrow a bunch of money you can't pay back, when starting out. Start small, count your pennies and make them all count. Keep your overhead as low as possible. Trust me, you will grow and get established before you know it. In other words Bloom where your Planted. Start Smart, Start Small and Enjoy the Ride to the Top.

MAKE A LIST OF EQUIPMENT
YOU WILL NEED.
THEN A LIST OF SECOND
HAND STORES WHERE
YOU'LL FIND WHAT YOU'LL NEED TO GET
STARTED.

STORES	EQUIPMENT

RESOURCES

RENAE ROLLINS

PROFEESIONAL COACHING SESSIONS
WORLD CLASS ACADEMY LIFE CLASS
MOTIVATIONAL SPEAKER
BOOKING: (850)404-4427
WEBSITE: WORLDCLASSACADEMYOFBEAUTYCAREERS.COM

RESOURCES

SUNBIZ.COM REGISTRY NWFLBBIC

BUSINESS LOANS ACCOUNTANT
IRS.GOV
BUSINESS & PROFESSIONAL RELGULATIONS/
FLORIDA MY FLORIDA.COM
THE CREDIT UNION

BE YOU

Never a Cheap copy. God has made only one of you.
Once Heee created you, he broke the mode!
Your fingerprints are Unique!
different from any one else's.
Your DNA is Different it's Only yours.

Be You.
Remember you are Fearfully and wonderfully made.
You are the one and only. The Original.
If they don't like you for who you Are
throw them a KISS GOODBYE!
Never change who you are to be someone else!
To be frank they really don't look that good on you!
Let that sit.
Why be their Copy?
Yes, a Fake?
Why be a "maybe" or just an "okay?"
Fake Louis Vuitton or Gucci are nice
but can't top the original design.
To feel the Original, the Authentic design
and being able to have the experience of
going into the actual Louis Vuitton or Gucci
Store to buy the Authentic Bag feels like no
other. There's quality, there's authenticity.
Let the world see the Authentic you.

Be all you can Be.
Do everything in Life that God
has placed in you to do!
Never! I mean Never Be a One Trick Horse!
We want Multiple Streams of Income. In order
to have that you must be authentic.

You must be you!
You've run this Race. You've Finished This Course!
Move on and start cutting, curling,
managing and starting your businesses.

You Can Do it!
Take it to the next Level!
Yesss! you are Originals made by the Best,
made with precision, made To last.
you may Bend But don't you ever Break!

You are Royalty!
Fight the Good Fight!

Because You Win in the End by
Being you

-RENAE ROLLINS

TESTIMONIALS

Nikayle Richardson
Cosmetologist/ Business owner

Coming into world class I was quite wide eyed and over-confident with things I thought I knew. If I was uncomfortable with a subject Id remain quiet and shy. However, if I knew.... Boy! I would butt heads with Mrs. Renae and other instructors because I believed I knew it all. One of the biggest lessons I've learned is to value and respect the relationship between teacher and student. I came in ready but anxious due to perfectionism. I wanted to execute every client's hair requests perfectly. Every hairstyle was not perfect because I failed to remember that I was a student and in a learning environment. With time this lesson from Mrs. Renae taught me how to face the reality and see things in a more mature way. She was always real with me and down to listen. Mrs. Renae gives you an opportunity to learn what it takes to be a business owner and hairstylist while in school. I've grown confident in my abilities during and after my time at World Class Academy of Beauty Careers. Mrs. Renae showed me the reality of being a stylist as well as the business of it all and for that I'm grateful.I came into World Class as young girl and graduated as a young woman.

Jacqulyn Rumph
Cosmetologist/ Business owner

"Stepping out on faith must be one of the most challenging experiences I've ever been through. The only two things that i was completely sure of is that i was unhappy with the position I was in & that I had nothing left to lose. Fast forward to now I'm living a lost & found dream of becoming a hairstylist. To those of you who are currently on your journey please know that it will not be easy, but it will be worth more than you could ever imagine. If at any time you begin to become weary, scared, or alone, always remember that God is right beside you every step of the way. Remeber that what you can't handle you can with him." "Tune in on your vision and begin to walk in a straight line towards it. People will leave, old habits will be no longer, and things will come and try to knock you off your path, but through it all remain focused on your vision and watch how God gives you everything that youve ask for and need." - Renae Rollins

Norman Caison
Cosmetologist/ Esthetician / Business owner

"All Journeys are meant to travel, All Test are meant to Test. It was always up to me to get myself to the next place. From lack of love, drugs, and even homelessness God still made a way. LIFE takes you places that you'd never image, like taking your Pressures to potential as if the pressures never happened. understanding that current situations were not my final destinations brought me so much life. That's why doing business on a dime is worth my time."

Ny'Asa Brantley
Cosmetologist/ Business owner

Greetings I'm here to humbly share my testimony with those who may be feeling lost or experiencing an identity crisis because they don't understand their God-given purpose. I wasn't as fortunate as a child; little did I know I was fortunate because I had what I needed; I was constantly on the move. My family made the best of it, which is why I'm grateful and full of love. My senior year, I ended up homeless due to a house fire right before my high school graduation and before I could start college at Florida Agricultural & mechanical University. I began failing classes, became distracted, and was on the verge of dropping out. I was surrounded by toxic relationships and friendships that served no purpose in my life. I began working as Mrs. Renae Rollins' secretary and am now a student at World class academy! Who would have guessed? I've asked myself this question several times, and through it all, I can only say BUT GOD! One day, I awoke inspired to learn more and to begin developing a deeper relationship with my Savior, Jesus Christ. I xpressed my feelings to my cosmetology instructor, which led to her sharing them with Mrs. Renae, she began life class! Her joy is contagious and spreads to those who listen. Her words of encouragement are motivating and genuine. Also. Mrs. Renae truly speaks from the heart, and you can tell she enjoys what she does. Delivering a powerful message that combines the two most important ingredients for life's success: FAITH in the Lord and FAITH in yourself! When you combine those two things with a positive attitude and a pair of optimistic glasses, you can not only improve your life, but also the lives of those around you! He is developing leaders! "I am not leading followers!"

Jakira M Scott

Designer Behind Doing Business on a Dime
Visual Artist / Senior Graphic Designer/ Cosmetologist/ Business owner

Before coming to World Class I had already started a business venture in visual arts and graphic design. I had professional achievements and the proper degrees to support my goals as well as additional experience in hosting events and traditional arts marketing. I've always been a curious person and sought out challenging and creative interests. Despite all my achievements throughout the years looking great on paper, I also had pre-existing trauma that I was dealing with at the time. Trauma that spawned behaviors like hypervigilance, overthinking and anxiously planning for the unknown. The habits that I developed made me feel safe and protected and I tried to work through them, but they also hindered me from achieving the goals that I was reaching for. I struggled with feelings of insufficiency, self doubt and crippling perfectionism. Even when it seemed as though everything was executed perfectly, it was never enough. I've always been Incredibly hard on myself and I've learned that this mentality is a serious weakness, but it can also be a surprising strength as well. It can push you to be great but hold you back at the same time because it's rooted in fear and not just in preparation. When I enrolled into world class Mrs. Renae saw this in me. She saw how this mentality kept me stagnant in my journey.

The only way to be a great swimmer is to get into the water. Based on how bad you want to live you could either learn to tread water and float like a master or drown from fear. Mrs. Renae and other instructors saw my attention to detail as a strength and soon, I began to doubt myself less. She saw how much I cared about the quality of what had my name attached to it and my unwavering dedication to see it through. So, much to my dismay I was thrown right into the thick of things and as difficult as it was, this strategy developed and nurtured my confidence. I learned to "do it scared" as it were. I learned that you must be confident in your own ability and firm in the fact that God's got you. He can take you where you need to be, even if all you have is talent and a dime to your name. I learned that life comes at you in many different ways, just like in a salon. I've learned to use my talent and attention to detail to prepare and do my best when the opportunity comes, knowing that I've done my best and not that I've done things perfectly. The truth is you can have all the talent in the world, but unsureness and a lack of confidence will keep you hidden. With that, I decided not to hide anymore.

Life Lessons

1. Be You it looks good on you!
2. Don't Follow People. Follow God. Always Listen and Hear from God!
3. Check it out for yourself. Don't just take what others tell you and run with it. Research it for yourself.
4. Remember what they told you. Never forget the Advice given to you!
5. Never Stop believing.
6. Let the Smoke Clear or let the dust settle. You will be ok when it does!
7. Don't be quick to Judge. You could be wrong!
8. Take time out for yourself. Take time to sharpen your iron and you'll come back stronger each time!
9. Give yourself a break. You will never be perfect!
10. Don't jump to conclusions. Wait it out!
11. Don't count your chickens before they hatch. Something could go wrong!
12. Free yourself from what they think or say. You will be better off!

13. Do the right thing no matter what. It really makes a difference!
14. Go with your Gut every time. It's usually right!
15. Do your Heart Work. If it's in your Heart, Do it!
16. Work Smarter not Harder
17. Listen, Watch and Pray
18. Read the fine print!
19. Have a Lawyer Friend. You'll need them!
20. Keep it Moving. Never stop, Never Give up and don't dwell on your Pass!
21. Write it Down, check it off and read it again!
22. Finish what you start.
23. Choose someone you can Help.
24. Live Freely
25. Dance
26. Begin with the end in mind.
27. Show up. You matter!
28. Use your gift, it will make room for you!
29. Hurry up and wait. Do what you can do now, then wait and watch it come together!
30. Make a Plan then Work it Out.
31. Nothing is Wasted. You'll be able to use it all. Every good and Bad thing will work for you!
32. Leave nothing on the Table. Every gift, Every talent, Every Idea and Everything that God's placed into your Spirit do it, try it and Leave Nothing on Table!

www.ingramcontent.com/pod-product-compliance
Lightning Source LLC
Chambersburg PA
CBHW031550210526
45464CB00003B/1235